Help for Self-Reliant Entrepreneur

85+ Free Remote Work Tools to Build
Trust, Communication, Projects,
Business Growth, and Inspirations to
Leap forward

I0480983

Ray Randy

Copyright

Disclaimer & Statement of Rights

The information presented herein represents the views of the author at the date of publication. Because medical researches and conditions continually change, the author reserves the right to change and update his opinions based on new conditions. Websites and references mentioned in this guide were all valid as at the time of producing this guide. This report is for informational purposes only and the author does not accept any responsibilities for any liabilities or damages, real or perceived, resulting from the use of this information.

TABLE OF CONTENTS

INTRODUCTION

There is no denying the fact that remote work has come to stay while its growth is being recorded every day. With the growth in the number of remote work, it has become very easy to own and operate an online business. This now leads to been overwhelmed with the volume of work that is caused by being an entrepreneur. This singular act is what differentiates between the struggling and the successful online business.

The discovery is that the struggling entrepreneur trying to keep up the pace with their work to move, the smart entrepreneurs make use of tools to make their work simple and get it done anywhere and around the world.

A common saying goes thus," an entrepreneur is as good as the tools he uses to run his business." If you are an entrepreneur that is yet to embrace using smart tools for your business, you may soon run out of business- as relying on the traditional way of work may not be ideal in this 21st century.

This is the reason why we have compiled a list of some smart tools for your business to leverage and run your business effectively. Some of these tools cover communication, collaboration, project management, Automation & Integration, List Building & Landing creation, to mention. The good things about all the tools mentioned in this book are for entrepreneurs on a low budget, and some are completely free.

Chapter 1

SOCIAL MEDIA MANAGEMENT & MARKETING

Presently most online entrepreneurs depend on social media engagement to enhance their brands and awareness to acquire more customers. No wonder it is important for business owners to be on top of their social media marketing plan. The following tools are essential if you want to make the marketing of your products online successful.

BUFFER

Buffer has been in the social media space to

help in making scheduling posts easy to do. Not only will it helps in the management of posts, but it also helps in the management of multiple profiles with no problem.

Buffer has many overlapping options, such as scheduling content while you are doing some work on the web with the help of its Chrome extensions (iOS, Android, Win, and Mac). Buffer will even suggest the right time to post your content based on your followers' activity from the same dashboard.

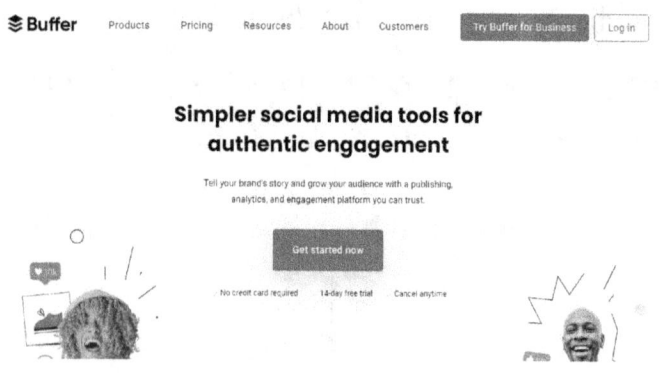

It has two categories: Publish and Analyze

For Publish it has three plans:

1. Pro:

Benefits: 8 social media accounts, 100 scheduled posts, and one user.

2. Premium:

Benefits: 8 social media accounts, 2000 scheduled posts, and two users

3. Business

Benefits: 25 social media accounts, 2000 scheduled posts, and six users.

For Analyze, it has two plans:

1. Pro:

Benefits: 8 Social media accounts, social analytics (in-depth), recommendations, and unlimited reports.

2. Premium: Benefits: 10 social media accounts,

analytics (inclusive stories), recommendations, unlimited reports, reports of White labeling, and Shopify integration.

Note: You can access Buffer for free for a 14-day trial without a credit card, and you have the option of canceling it anytime if you are not satisfied.

(https://buffer.com/)

HOOTSUITE

Hootsuite is a great social media manager that helps in managing content easily. From a single dashboard of Hootsuite, you will be able to schedule all your social media content and measure each social media account's performance.

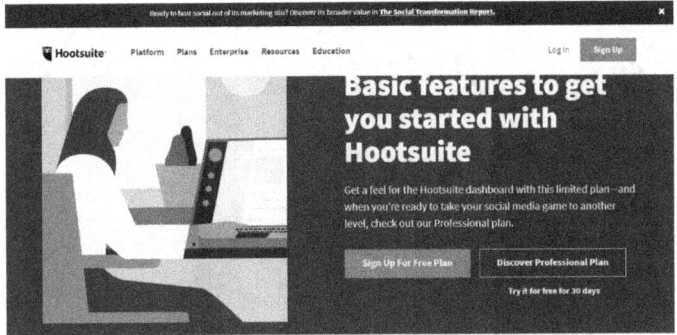

Hootsuite has two plans; free and the Paid plan.

Free Plan:

Benefits: 3 Social media accounts, 30 Scheduled posts, and generation of leads with social contests. It also includes basic analytics to monitor followers and growth, statistics of your content, and two RSS feed integration.

The paid category has four plans:

1. Professional.

Benefits: 10 social media profiles, unlimited scheduling, and accessible to 1 user.

2. Team.

Benefits: 20 social media profiles, unlimited scheduling, and three users.

3. Business.

Thirty-five social media profiles, unlimited scheduling, and more than five users.

Note: you can enjoy a free 30-day trial on all the paid plans.

(https://hootsuite.com/plans/free)

MISSINGLETTR

MissingLettr is an excellent AI online tool that will help you run an automated social media campaign, drive traffic to your profile for up to a year. Yours is just to set up your campaign, relax, and wait for the magical trends that will enhance your business.

Features on the platform are Automatic Social Campaigns, Optimized Social Content, Promote Guest Posts, Hashtag Recommendations, and many more.

It has two plans: Solo and Pro.

Solo:

Benefits: 1 site, two social profiles, 500 scheduled posts, and accessible to 1 user.

Pro:

Benefits: 3 sites, nine social profiles, 3000 scheduled posts, and access to unlimited users.

Note: Note: you can enjoy a free 30-day trial on all the plans.

(https://missinglettr.com/#)

TWEETDECK

If you use twitter for social media strategy, it will not be business-wise if you do not use TweetDeck. TweetDeck is the best social engagement dashboard on twitter. TweetDeck allows you to use custom timelines, create the ability to manage your lists, searches, and add more teams to your account. All these features are free on TweetDeck. Though TweetDeck is not all in one tool for your social media strategy, if you have more than one account on Twitter, TweetDeck is your answer in managing the accounts.

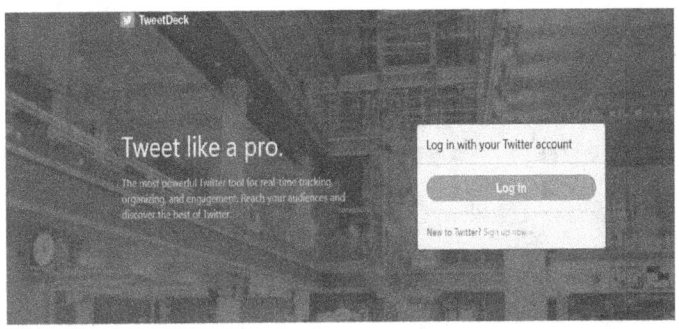

(https://tweetdeck.twitter.com/)

SOCIALOOMPH

SocialOomph has a wide range of options if you are having multiple platforms. Options such as scheduling posts, analytics, increase followers and help in keeping the DM Twitter inbox clean. Not only is SocialOomph for Twitter, but it also has features for Facebook, Pinterest, and LinkedIn.

SocialOomph has both a free plan and paid plans, but the free plan features are limited and tend towards twitter management. Despite the limitation, the following features are available to the free plan users, scheduling tweets, the ability to track your keywords, shorten URL's, and the ability to manage up to 5 Twitter accounts.

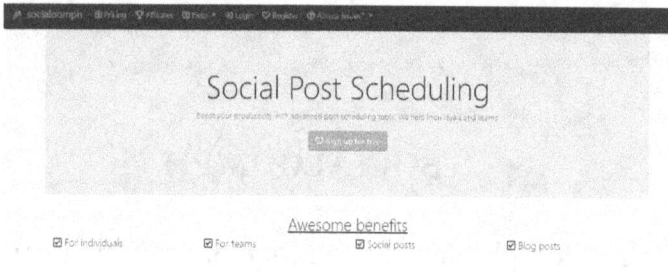

(https://www.socialoomph.com/)

ZOHO SOCIAL

It does not matter whether you are an entrepreneur or just an agency. Zoho Social is an excellent tool that will help you manage your multiple profiles, find relevant keywords, work with other team members, and schedule posts from one platform.

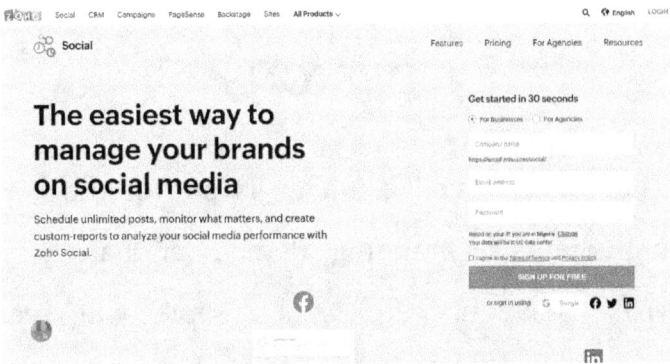

Zoho Social has features that other platforms in the same category have. Still, it comes with special features such as Facebook lead ads, reporting features (advanced), CRM integration, browser plugin (SocialShare).

Zoho Social has a free plan, but it is limited to managing one profile, using the browser plugin and URL shortener.

(https://www.zoho.com/social/)

Chapter 2

DESIGN

The use of visual elements is one of the key ingredients of branding. Remember that these visual elements are what people will see, recognize, and associate with before having business dealing with you. So it is reasonable to add outstanding visual elements to your brands.

Though many graphic designers will help you create fantastic designs, there may be a time when what you need to design is urgent, and there is room for a long time. So with this in mind, there are many free tools you can easily rely on to create stunning designs such as logos and flyers, even if you don't have a budget to hire professional graphics designers.

CANVA

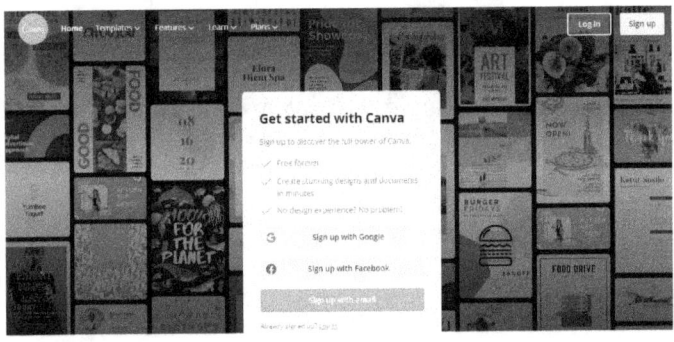

With Canva, you have the liberty of creating stunning designs for your business. Canva is a drag and drop platform to design logos, business cards, covers, presentations, and many more. Canva comes with an endless library of templates where you can choose what you need for your designs. You can use Canva on mobile devices and computers.

Other tools that come with it are Canva Photo Editor, Canva Font Combination, and Canva Generator.

There are two plans on Canva, free and paid.

The free plan is enough to do your basic designs, but you can go for the paid plan if you want advanced design templates and artworks.

(https://www.canva.com/)

PLACEIT

There are moments when you will need a photo for your blog, website, or Pinterest profile with a little bit of polish? PlaceIt is a better place to polish your design and create beautiful designs. Simply upload your photos to the site and see how your screenshots will turn to awesome designs. PlaceIt comes with ready to use templates both for free and paid users.

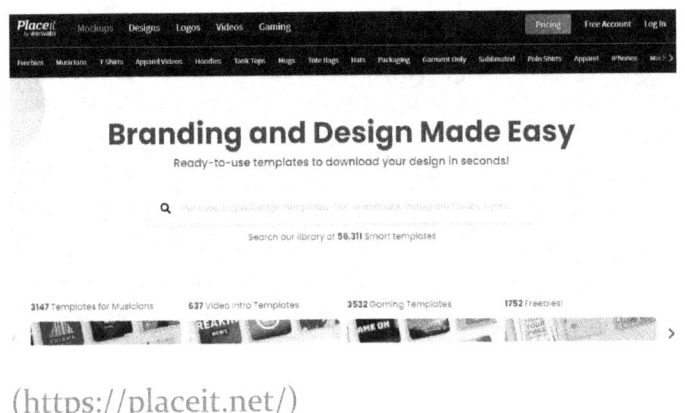

(https://placeit.net/)

SQUARESPACE LOGO MAKER

Use this site to create a beautiful and professional logo within a minute.

Squarespace logo maker is a free tool where you choose from thousands of logo templates to create a business logo.

(https://www.squarespace.com/logo#)

UNSPLASH

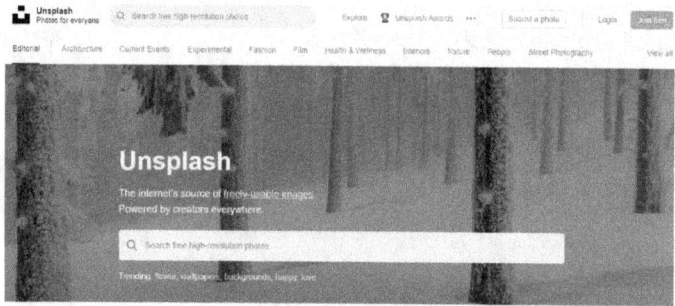

This is a site where you choose free images and photos for any of your projects. All the images and photos on this site are free and have no copyright issues.

(https://unsplash.com/)

WHATTHEFONT

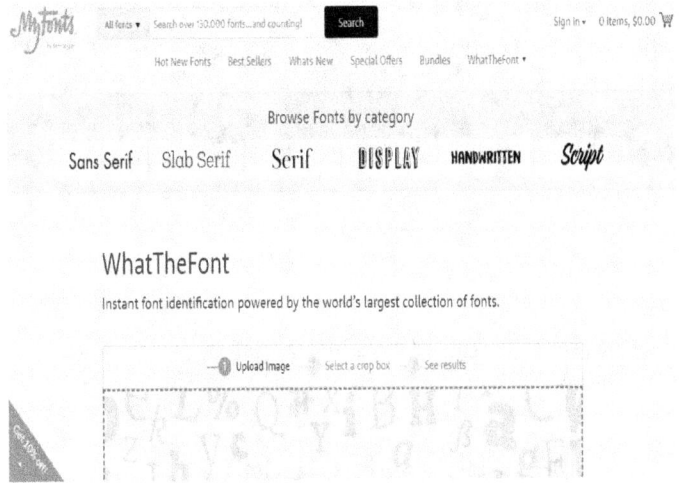

With this site, you can know a font you see somewhere and be able to use it. Simply upload the font's image to WhatTheFont, the said font and those that are closest to the font will be displayed on your screen.

(https://www.myfonts.com/WhatTheFont/)

FONT SQUIRREL

What Font Squirrel does it to quickly scour the internet and help you get high quality and free fonts? On this site, you can download thousands of free, quality, and legal fonts.

(https://www.fontsquirrel.com/)

AWESOME SCREENSHOT

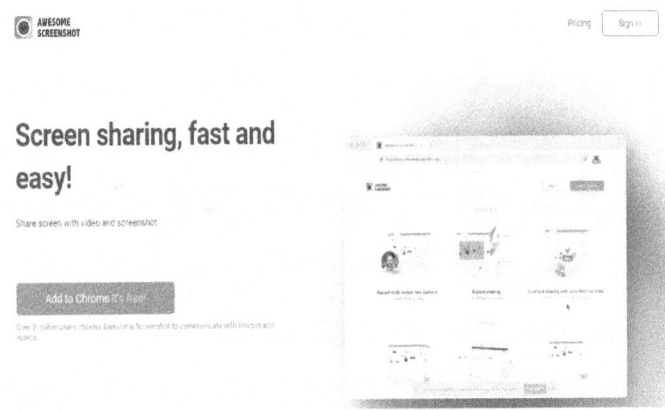

Have you found yourself trying to crop, annotate, and edit more than ten screenshots? With an Awesome screenshot that has extensions for both Firefox and Chrome, you will easily screenshot them on the website and edit them within the browser. It has free and paid plans.

(https://www.awesomescreenshot.com/)

SKITCH

Get your point across with fewer words using annotation, shapes and sketches, so that your ideas become reality faster.

Skitch is a handy screen capture tool from Evernote. It is a functional tool to help entrepreneurs and marketers get to their prospects with few words. With Skitch, you can use arrow, shapes, doodles, and texts to annotate your captured images and keep them either to your device or to your Evernote account for later use. It comes with free and paid plans.

(https://evernote.com/products/skitch)

LIGHTROOM (MOBILE)

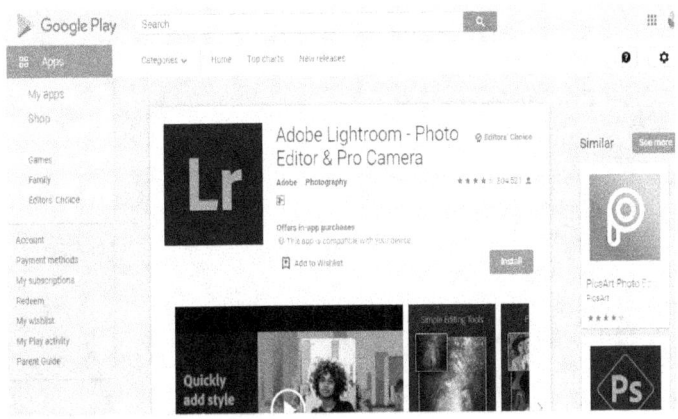

If you are not within reach of your computer or decide to edit a photo on a mobile device, Lightroom is a better option. With this app, you can edit your photo without losing the quality of the photos.

(https://play.google.com/store/apps/details?id=com.adobe.lrmobile&hl=en_US)

HUBSPOT'S 15 INFOGRAPHIC TEMPLATES

15 Free Infographic Templates in Powerpoint (+ 5 Bonus Illustrator Templates)

Save countless hours by using these pre-made templates to design your infographics.

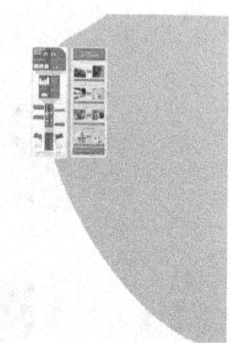

Download Now for Free

It is important to know how to create visual content. But in all honesty, most times, creating beautiful graphics can be huge, especially if you are not a professional graphic designer.

Hubspot comes with this pack of 15 free infographics templates that you can use to create infographics within a short time. The most advantage of this pack is that the template can be customized to suit your brand.

(https://www.hubspot.com/infographic-templates)

HUBSPOT'S 4 POWERPOINT SLIDESHARE TEMPLATES

You want to use SlideShare, but you don't know how to create them. Worry not as Hubspot has created free PowerPoint templates you can use as Slide Share presentations without stress.

Simply download the templates, and adjust to suit your brand.

(https://offers.hubspot.com/templates-create-beautiful-powerpointso)

Chapter 3

OUTSOURCING

Outsourcing is the kind of business where you hire an outsider from your team to perform services or create products that are supposed to be performed by your team members.

Outsourcing has become a major trend in recruiting over some past decades. As an entrepreneur, you will need to outsource some services and create goods to reduce your payroll and overhead costs.

At the outsourcing sites, you will be surprised at the avalanched of talents that are freelancers. Note that there will be times in the course of your business when you will need to outsource some of your work. The following are some of the best freelance sites.

FIVERR

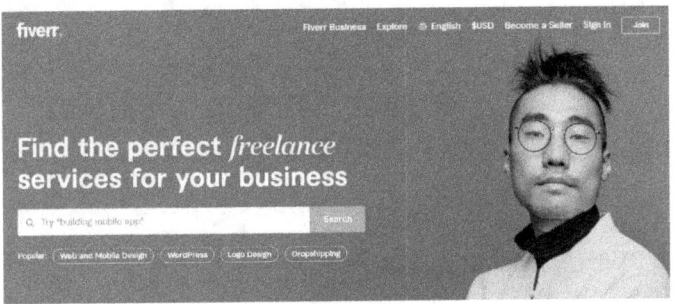

Here at Fiverr, the professionals post their works, you the buyer will review the jobs or gigs if it complies with the job to be given. The next is to contact the freelancer, and the work starts immediately. On this site, people with limited budgets can outsource their works for as little as $5.

(https://www.fiverr.com/)

UPWORK

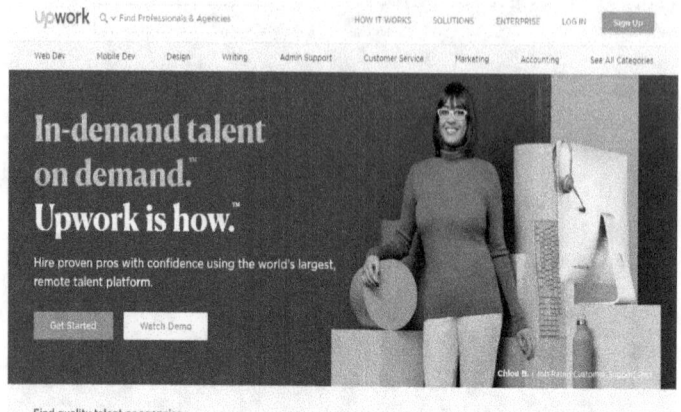

Find quality talent or agencies

Upwork will pay the verified time a freelancer spent on working for you. This is a site where you will find numerous competent professionals in all fields. Name it from writers to programmers to graphic designers, are on Upwork to work with you either for a one-time or long-time project.

(https://www.upwork.com/)

FREELANCER

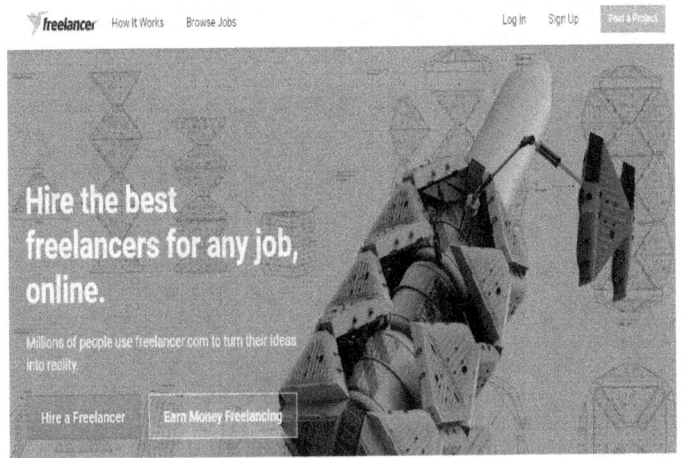

On Freelancer, you hire a competent professional worker, and you will need to create a payment milestone. The rule is as milestones are completed, the payment of the job done will be released. You will be surprised at the numbers of professionals that will want to do the job for you. Check their reviews and give your work to the best among them.

(https://www.freelancer.com/)

GURU

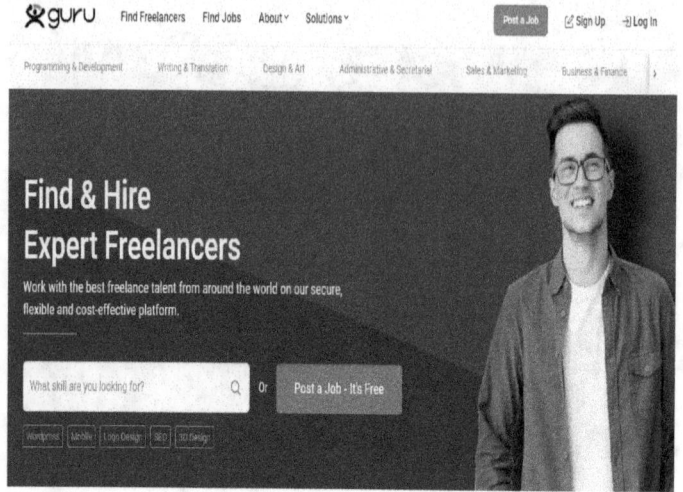

Here you find and hire expert freelancers around the world. The Website is secured, flexible, and cost-effective. You only pay for the completed work. The largest workers on this site are United States Americans.

(https://www.guru.com/)

AMAZON'S MECHANICAL TURK

Amazon Mechanical Turk (MTurk) is a crowdsourcing marketplace that makes it easier for individuals and businesses to outsource their processes and jobs to a distributed workforce who can perform these tasks virtually. This could include anything from conducting simple data validation and research to more subjective tasks like survey participation, content moderation, and more. MTurk enables companies to harness the collective intelligence, skills, and insights from a global workforce to streamline business processes, augment data collection and analysis, and accelerate machine learning development.

While technology continues to improve, there are still many things that human beings can do much more effectively than computers, such as moderating content, performing data deduplication, or research. Traditionally, tasks like this have been accomplished by hiring a large temporary workforce, which is time consuming, expensive and difficult to scale, or have gone undone. Crowdsourcing is a good way to break down a manual, time-consuming project into smaller, more manageable tasks to be completed by distributed workers over the Internet (also known as microtasks).

Amazon Mechanical Turk affords developers access to competent professionals with UI with the aid of a simple API. Some organizations have used crowdfunding through Amazon's Mechanical Turk for help with objectives such as machine learning development, microwork, and human insight.

On this site, you, the job owner, will decide the amount you want to pay for the job to be done.

(https://www.mturk.com/)

Chapter 4

COMMUNICATION, COLLABORATION & PROJECT MANAGEMENT

You know the number of emails and call you to exchange with your team every day, and how long it takes to brief them on goals and progress. If your answers to these make you cringe, then it is better to update your collaboration tools.

Understand that collaboration will not work if there is no proper communication. There must be communication from instant messaging to video conference.

After you have established good communication, there will easy collaboration that may lead to better management of the project together.

ZOOM

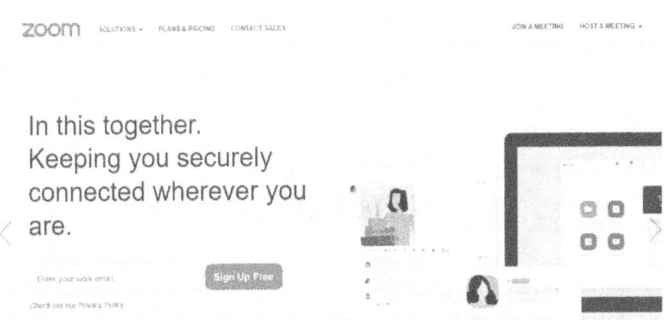

Zoom is a cloud-based video conferencing software you can make use to meet other people virtually. This software can connect up to 500 people together online either by video or audio-video or both for webinars, meetings, and conferences. Zoom affords the opportunity to record the conference to be able to view later.

Zoom comes in two main plans; free and paid

plans. The free plan affords you the opportunity to host up to 100 people, 40 minutes max for group meetings, and unlimited 1 and 1 meetings.

(https://zoom.us/)

MICROSOFT TEAMS

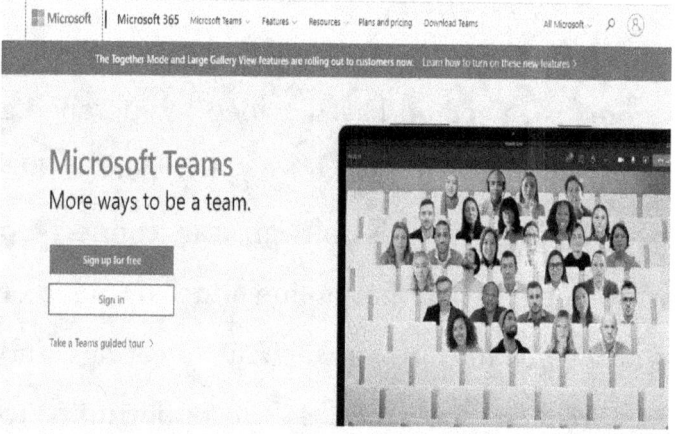

Microsoft Teams is a chat-based collaboration platform that allows global, remote, and teams that are not together with the opportunity to work together and be able to share information through a common space.

It comes with features such as document collaboration, team chat, 1 and 1 chat, and more. This tool is integrated fully into some Office 365 services that include yammer, Skype, SharePoint, and Exchange.

Microsoft Teams comes with free and paid plans. The free plan comes with benefits such as unlimited chat and search, collaboration in real-time with Office, online meetings and video calling, and team and personal file storage.

(https://www.microsoft.com/en-us/microsoft-365/microsoft-teams/free)

GOOGLE MEET

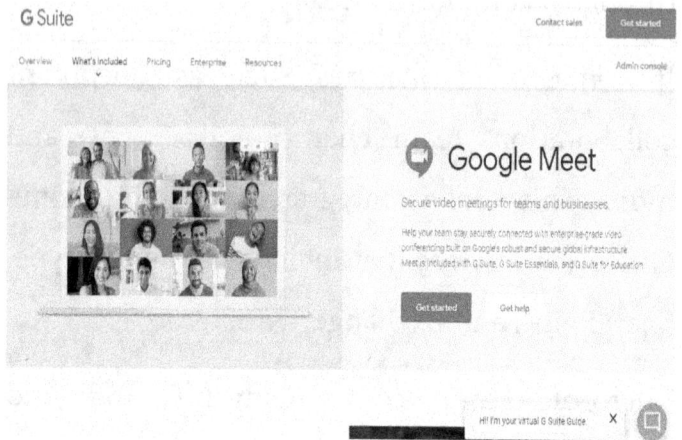

Google Meet is a video-conference calling tool created for professional use that links remote colleagues together for interaction. It was Google Hangouts that was upgraded to Google Meet. You can use this tool for webinars and online meetings.

To set up Google Meet, you have to first have a paid version of the G Suite account that costs $6 per month on a basic level. But to join, you need a Google account and participate in the Google Meet.

(https://gsuite.google.com/intl/en/products/meet)

SLACK

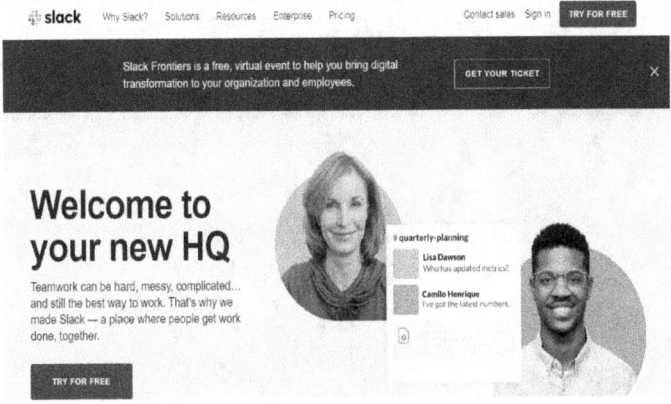

Slack is a popular and well-crafted communication platform that offers instant messaging, message search, and file transfer. With Slack, you will be able to create activities that will fast track your work, such as tasks, objectives, and goals. Slack is designed such a way to integrate with other communication apps like Trello, to give better collaboration experience.

(https://slack.com/intl/en-ng/)

BASECAMP

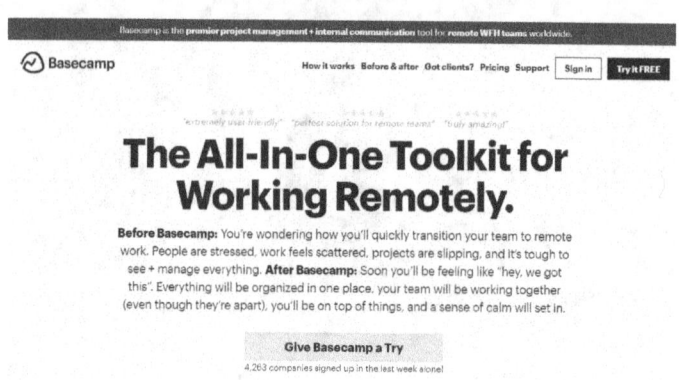

Basecamp is a real-time project and communication tool that aids teams in organizing projects on the same page. It comes with features such as to-do lists, file sharing, due dates, and calendaring. Basecamp helps the teams to keep what is going on as actionable items and priorities. It has a way of constantly updating every team member about the tasks or projects they are working on presently.

Basecamp is 100% free and is designed for freelancers, families, students, and organizations.

(https://basecamp.com/)

TRELLO

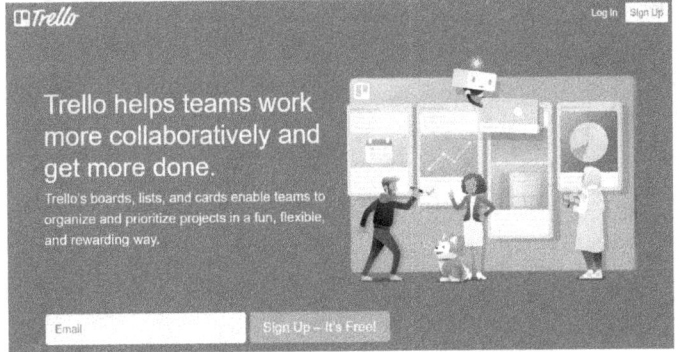

Trello is a project management tool that can best be used to organized projects or tasks and assign them to each team member, and at the same time, monitor the progress of their work. Trello is excellent in planning, brainstorming, and designing the activities that will be shared among the team members so for the goal to be achieved faster.

(https://trello.com/)

ASANA

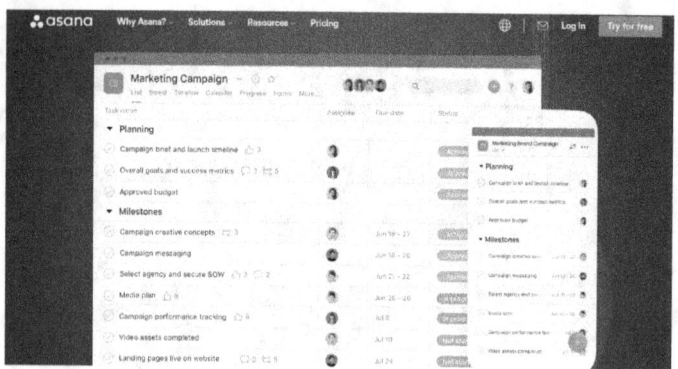

When talking about project management tools, only a few among all will beat Asana. With Asana, you will be able to break your project into tasks. It comes with project tracking, video calls, and integrations such as reminders, to-do lists, and direct requests. Don't forget that you can use Asana to track and monitor the progress of the ongoing projects. Asana is free for up to 15 people, and there is a paid plan.

(https://asana.com/product)

Chapter 5

LINK SHORTENER

Nobody wants to click a link that is long, boring, and unattractive. There is this CTA that normally happens when people see a short and catchy link. We discovered that most entrepreneurs find it very difficult to create unique and branded links to have a converted call to action to their products, services, and websites. The following tools are excellent when it comes to shortening your links to catchy types.

BIT.LY

We discovered that Bit.ly is the best of all the

link shorteners you can get on the internet. This tool affords you to either shortened and customize your links, as you may wish. Not only is Bit.ly a link shortener, but it can also help in tracking some useful information that includes where the link is most clicked.

It comes in free and paid plans. To only get your link to shorten, the free version will do that for you, but to brand your links, you will need to get the paid plan.

(https://bitly.com/)

REBRANDLY

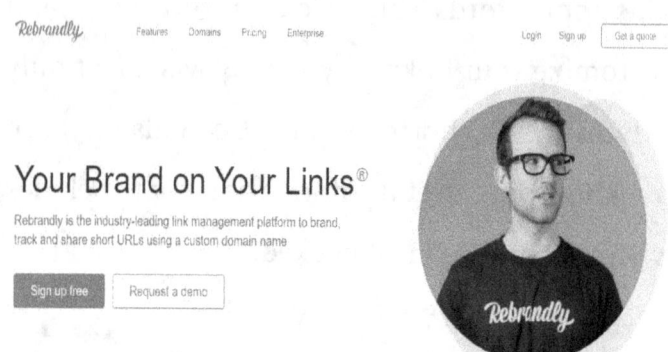

Rebrandly is another excellent tool for links shortener. This tool can also help in turning long links into short and branded links. It will also help in tracking where the clicks on the links are coming from. So Rebrandly is a great online marketing tool for entrepreneurs. It comes in free and paid plans.

(https://www.rebrandly.com/)

TINYURL

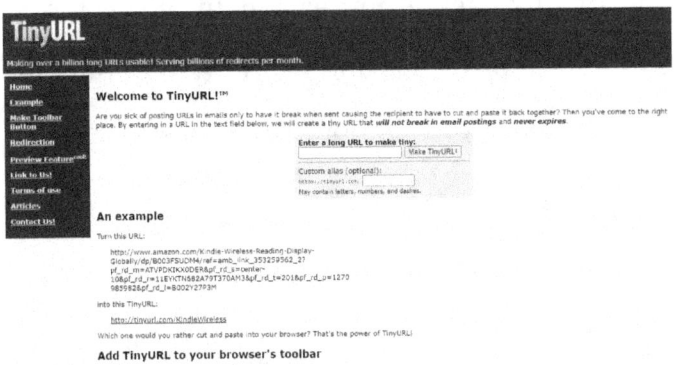

TinyURL is for entrepreneurs on a low budget as it is completely free. This tool has been on the internet since 2002, and it is good whenever you are in a hurry to create short links. Another advantage of this tool is that it will even suggest a shorter URL, and you the ability to customize it. Not only is this tool for link shortener, but it will also offer you to add a bookmarklet to the web browser's toolbar that will generate a short link from the webpage just by clicking the button. This clicking will lead you to where to get the link back. Another benefit of this tool is that it is anonymous and will never contain any reports about your or your links.

(https://tinyurl.com)

HYPERLINK

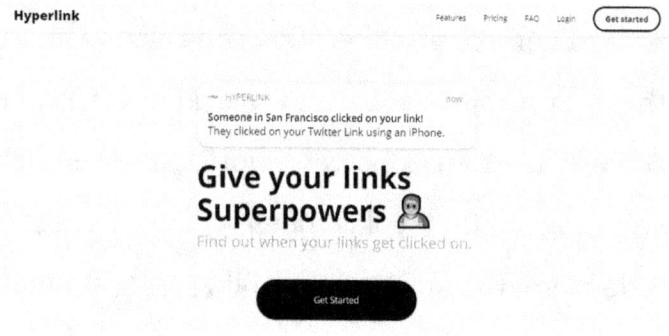

The Hyperlink is a link shortener that works best with mobile. This tool has Android and iOS apps that are great and work excellently. However, it also has a chrome extension that you can add to your browser, and it will work perfectly. Hyperlink's main benefit is that once you have its app on your mobile or extension on your browser, you will be receiving notifications of where the clicks on your links are coming from. You even have the opportunity to tell the Hyperlink to organize the delivery of the notification to hourly, daily, or weekly if the delivery of the notifications is getting out of hands. Another benefit of Hyperlink is the ability to help you track and analyze your audience and their locations.

It comes in free and paid plans.

(https://usehyperlink.com/)

Chapter 6

BLOGGING

A blog is just like a website. A blog is a kind of website where you organize content in the form of posts and categories. It has pages to organize your information, and through the posts, you have the liberty to market your goods and services.

Making good use of your blog is blogging. You use blogging in online business to capture emails, acquire new leads, engage with the audience, and offer new goods and services to your audience.

Some blog posts are Personal blog, Personal Brand blog, Corporate Blog, Personal Services

Blog, Niche Blog, Affiliate Blog, Guest Blogs, and more.

The following sites are where you can go to even if you are on a low budget to start blogging.

WORDPRESS

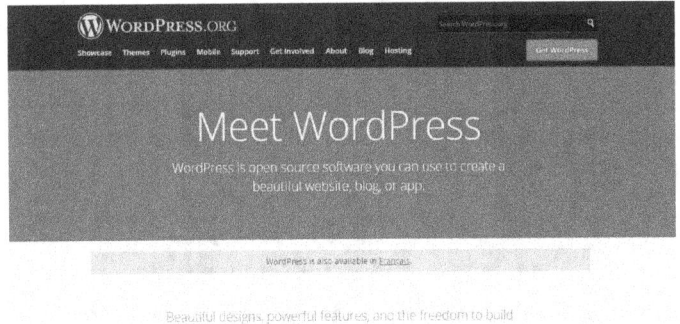

WordPress, without mincing words, is the king of free blogging sites. What you need is you have to build the site by yourself once your domain name has been approved. With

Wordpress.org, you host the site yourself, and you may decide later to find paid hoisting if you want to make your blog a long-term plan. WordPress offers you tons of themes, plugins, and templates to make your sites beautiful and catchy.

(https://wordpress.org/)

WIX

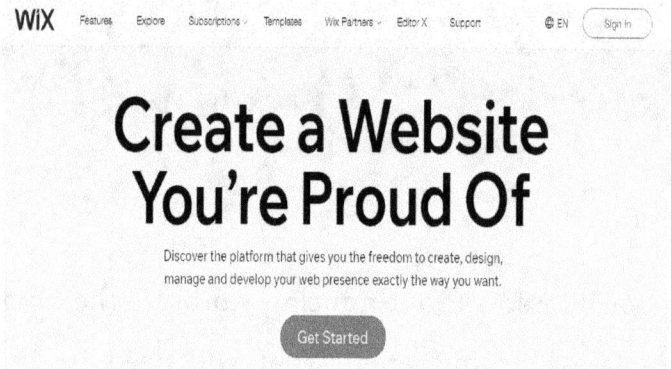

Wix is also a free website builder that is easy to

manage from the front-end. This website builder's unique selling point is that it comes with drag and drop features that will handle everything in the back-end. Just like WordPress, Wix also has free hosting; yours is to arrange your layouts, choose a template, and you are good to go. Wix comes with free and premium templates and themes for various projects.

Sign up on the website and start creating your site, or you can allow the Wix AI to create a stunning site for you based on the questions it asks.

(https://www.wix.com/)

MEDIUM

Medium is a platform where you have the ability to track different topics. The deal is this, create an account, and start to write on any type of topic you decide on. Medium's main benefit over other blog sites is that your articles will be exposed to many audiences. This site has more than 60 million people visiting it every time. The Medium disadvantage is that your articles are on the Medium, and you are not building your site like WordPress or Wix.

(https://medium.com/)

BLOGGER

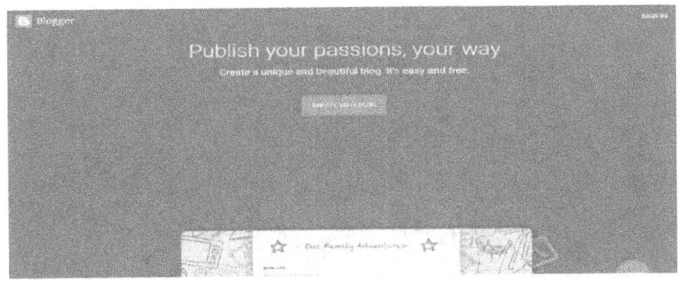

Blogger is the oldest of all the free blog sites, though its popularity comes down in recent years. Blogger, presently with the introduction of new blog sites, has been discovered not to be the best resource for professional use. Sign up with the Blogger, pick your preferred theme from the default, and start blogging.

(https://www.blogger.com/about/)

TUMBLR

Tumblr is one of the great blogging sites on the web, as it is milder and is mainly created for publishing purposes. The site interface is interesting to work with. Simply sign up and begin to post. Tumblr affords you different ways to post your content, but it is mainly for personal use and may not be the best for business-oriented strategy.

(https://www.tumblr.com/)

Chapter 7

LIST BUILDING & LANDING PAGE CREATION

With all the tools listed below, you will be able to design a site, collect leads, sales pages, and have more audiences, even if you are not the type that knows how to create and design websites. Even if you are on a low budget with the tools listed, you will be able to create beautiful and high-converting landing pages to have more audience to be able to grow your business. Though there are well-known paid tools with more sophisticated options than the ones presented below, you will be able to grow your business with the following tools.

CONVERTKIT

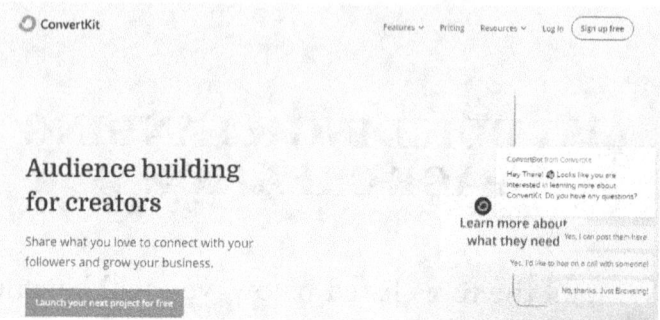

With ConvertKit, you will be able to launch your landing pages and begin to collect emails for free. This tool will allow you to manage 1000 subscribers, the ability to have unlimited landing pages and forms, customizable domain, unlimited traffic, and more for free. Simply sign up and choose the theme you want to use for the landing page. ConvertKit allows you to organize a meeting, verify your next business idea, gather a list for your online course, and

host an online workshop. It comes with free and paid plans.

(https://convertkit.com/)

UCRAFT

Free landing page builder by Ucraft

Build responsive landing pages to showcase your product,
drive organic traffic and generate more leads.
A little personal touch and you are all set.

See all templates ↓

Ucraft is a website builder designed to create landing pages for free and target small business owners, bloggers, and online entrepreneurs. It is a drag and drop platform, so there is no need to learn any coding to create beautiful landing pages. Ucraft comes with free and paid plans, but the free version has 18 templates you can choose from. This tool is easy to use, and you can upgrade to the paid version if you want to enjoy some other benefits.

(https://www.ucraft.com/free-landing-page-creator)

CARRD

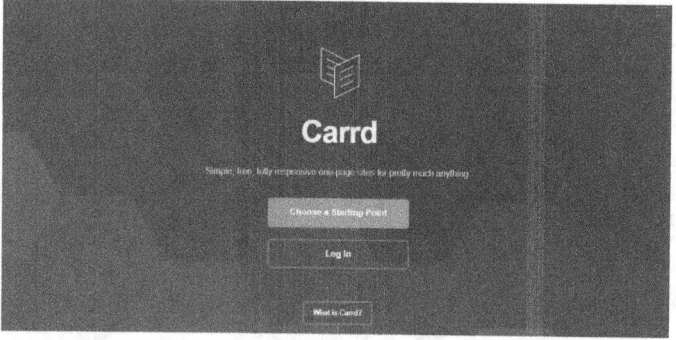

The Carrd is discovered to be more than a free landing page builder. It is a powerful platform to create simple and responsive sites. Once you sign up on Carrd, you will be able to create personal profiles, portfolios, landing pages, various signup pages, and more. It comes with different kinds of templates, and you are good to go. On the Carrd, it is very easy to add videos, texts, images, links, and forms. The Carrd comes in free and paid plans, but when on a free plan, you will not be able to include a Signup form or Contact form.

(https://carrd.co/)

LAUNCHROCK

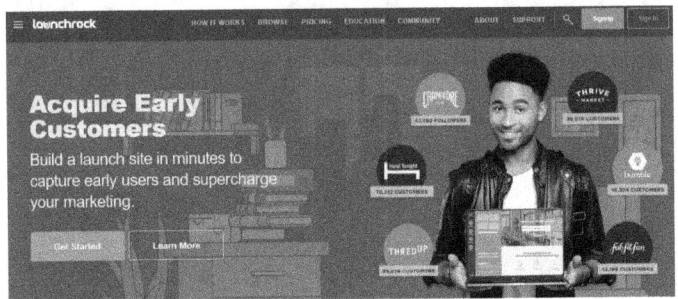

Do you know that Launchrock is part of the startups.com that offers different courses, podcasts, a community of startup founders, and online creators? So Launchrock is of the few tools they created to help business owners in creating a new site and acquire more clients. Simply Signup, and create a new site in Launchrock, and you are good to go. The platform is designed in such a way as it will allow you to select if you are launching a service, product, event, or mobile app. Next is to add the name and select the preferred template. Add texts, titles, landing page copy, and more. It comes with free and paid plans, but presently there are no major differences between the free and paid plans.

(https://www.launchrock.com/)

LANDBOT

Landbot is entirely different from other landing pages builders, as it is not a static type of builder. Still, it affords the opportunity to create interactive, conversational landing pages that will not only engage your visitors but also guide them through joining the list for the lead magnet, product, or webinar. It is created with a chatbot that will guide through the creation of the account. You select between Elegant and

Casual styles for the landing page and customize to soothe your purpose. Landbot comes with free and paid plans, but the free plan limits you to 100 chats in a month and only 30 blocks inside each bot. A free user can also make use of the Zapier integration that will add the leads to existing email service provider or CRM automatically.

(https://landbot.io/)

Chapter 8

EMAIL MARKETING, AUTOMATION & CRM

The following Marketing automation and CRM tools are

It is a great way for business owners to save money or those on a low budget to get their businesses on tracks. These tools are important options for a modern business if you want to grow in profit. With these tools, you will create an automated workflow, newsletters, email campaigns, customer relationships, and many more. All the tools listed below are in free plans, but I will rather advise that if you want to enjoy these tools' full functions, it is better to go for the paid plans.

MAILCHIMP

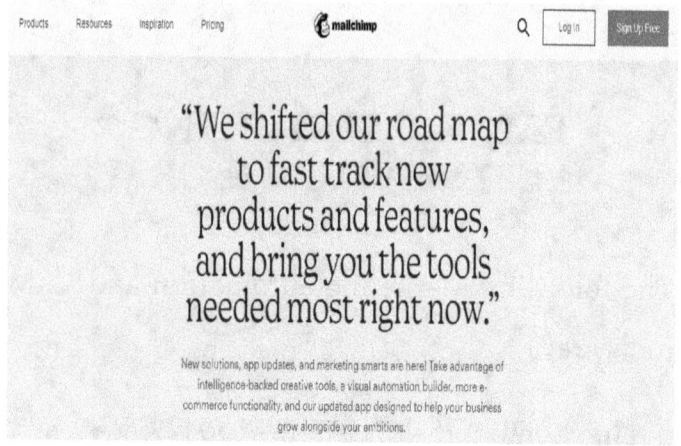

The MailChimp is a comprehensive marketing automation tool with a wide range of options. As a free user, you have access to 2000 contacts, Forms & Landing Pages, MailChimp Domain, Marketing CRM, Website Builder, and Creative Assistant. The paid plans come with other advanced benefits.

(https://mailchimp.com)

SENDER

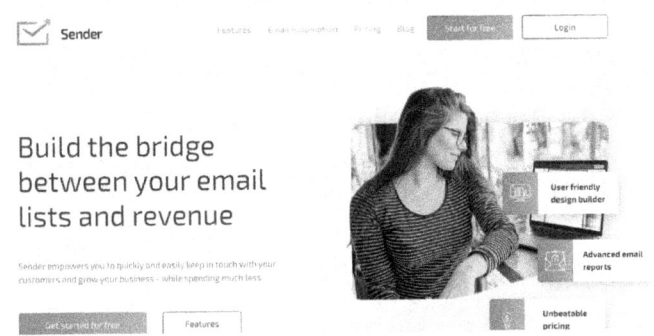

The Sender is another great marketing automation software that provides many options, focusing on visual appeal and simplicity when it comes to usage. This tool is designed for the users to have access to free newsletter templates and drag and drop editor. All the templates are compatible with email clients, and the newsletter looks beautiful and catchy on all mobile devices. With the Sender, you have the opportunity to track who opened the emails and be able to optimize your campaigns to who and when. The Sender comes in free and paid plan, but you have access to 2500 subscribers and up to 15000 emails per month to the free plan.

(https://www.sender.net)

MAILERLITE

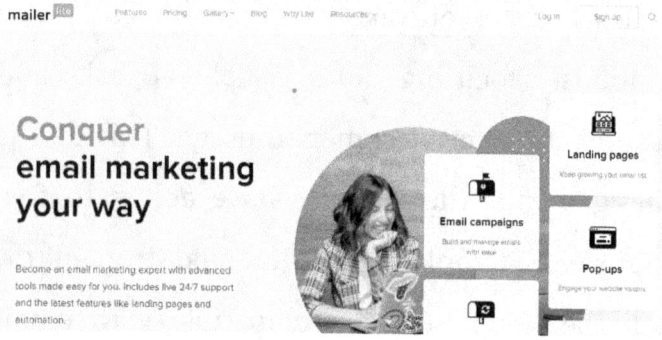

The MailerLite is another comprehensive email marketing automation software that helps entrepreneurs grow subscribers and build strong relationships. It comes with drag and drops editor, HTML editor, rich text editor, and many more. With the MailerLite, you will be able to create landing pages, create embedded pop-ups forms, and manage your subscribers to get their attention. The MailerLite comes in free and paid plans. But with a free plan, you have access to 1000 subscribers, 12000 emails per month, landing pages, embedded signup forms, pop-ups forms, and more.

(https://www.mailerlite.com)

HUBSPOT

The Hubspot is one of the biggest vendors when it comes to Salesforce, and it gives free CRM unlimited to their users with basic options. With free Hubspot CRM, you will be able to assign and track leads, manage your project workflow, manage the sales, and record customer interactions. The CRM tools available to free users are contact management, Deals, Contact website activity, Companies, Tasks & activities, Meeting

Scheduling, Email templates, and more.

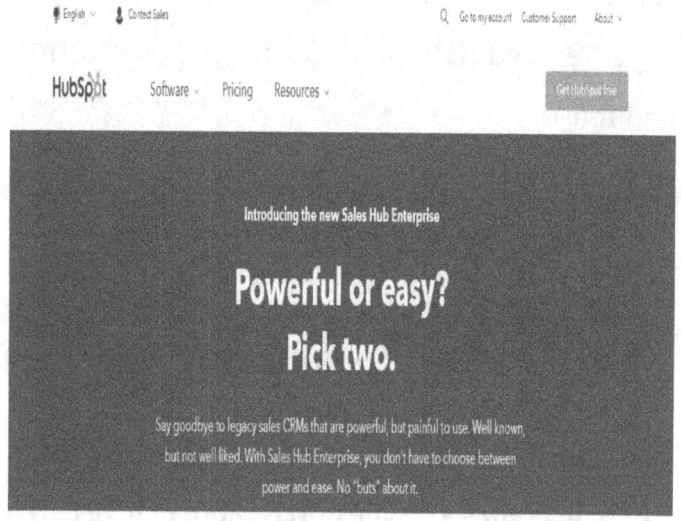

(https://www.hubspot.com)

BITRIX24

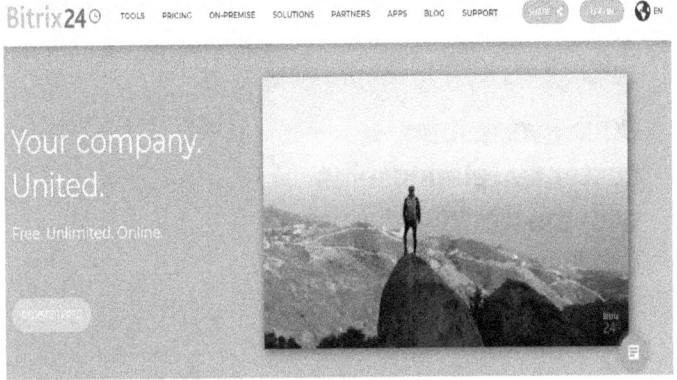

Bitrix24 is one of the popular CRM in the world based on the number of business owners using it. This tool provides free CRM solutions for 12 users with online storage of 5 GB, Communications, and tasks and projects. Other things you will enjoy are lead management, pipeline management, reporting, task automation, and more. It also comes with a paid plan.

(https://www.bitrix24.com/)

ZOHO

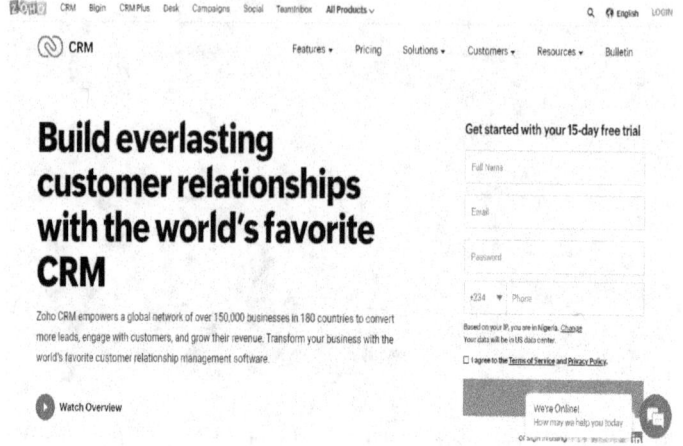

The Zoho CRM created a good platform for small business owners with a simple user interface, social media options, automation, and more. The free plan allows only three users and will afford you to build up and specify your workflow, manage your leads, and organize your day-to-day activities. Zoho CRM is integrated with Google+, Twitter, and Facebook. It is advisable to upgrade to Zoho's paid plan to enjoy other advanced benefits that come with it.

(https://www.zoho.com/crm/)

Chapter 9

FILE MANAGEMENT & SHARING

It is now extremely easy due to the internet for anyone to save and share their cloud-based files. It does not matter the kinds of person you are-be it business owner, freelancer, employee, or you want to share documents or videos with friends, family, or associates. Saving and sharing cloud-based files is now a thing of a single click. The tools listed below are some of the best free File Management & Sharing tools you can use on the internet.

GOOGLE DRIVE

Google Drive from Google.com is the most popular of all the file management and sharing tools on the internet. It allows you to save and share files that include documents, images, videos, and anything than can be saved or shared on the internet. You can access the files saved in Google Drive anywhere and anytime on any type of internet compliance device in the world. Just log into your Google Drive account, and you are good to go. Google Drive affords the free users 15 GB of cloud-based to save all your files, but you will have to purchase more space if you need more. This tool also comes in apps that can be operated on mobile devices.

(https://www.google.com/drive/)

AMAZON DRIVE

Amazon has cloud-based storage for consumers that was formerly known as Amazon Cloud Drive, but now Amazon Drive. With Amazon

Drive, users will be able to store their videos, photos, documents, and more to the Amazon's cloud and access it anywhere and anytime in the world. With this tool apps that can be operated on mobile devices, you can set the Drive into Auto-Save to back up the files on the mobile devices. If you are an Amazon Prime member, Amazon Drive will give you 5GB to store your files on the cloud, but if you want a 1TB plan, you will have to pay $60.

(https://www.amazon.com/b/?node=1554713001 1)

DROPBOX

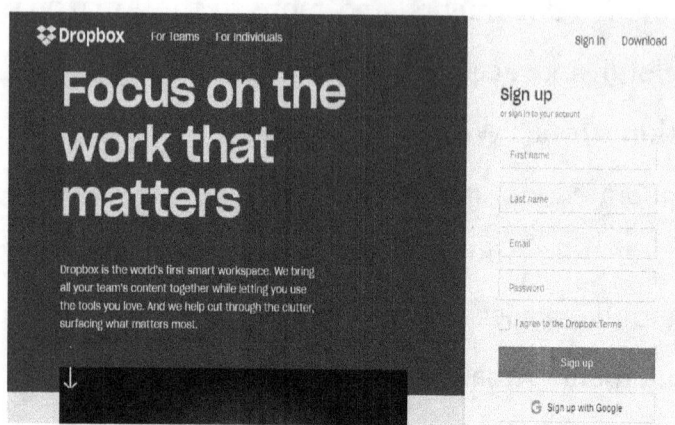

Online file management and sharing with Dropbox have become another great thing. Dropbox is another giant tool like Google Drive when it comes to the storage of files to the cloud. Not only will Dropbox store your files, but it will also give you desktop clients and mobile app that will help you in keeping your files intact and within reach. Dropbox gained popularity due to its simple interface design, reliable servers, desktop clients, mobile apps, and many more. With Dropbox, you can integrate with more than 100,000 third-party apps making it a factory for cloud storage. However, only 2GB storage is given to free users, not what Google Drive offers.

(https://www.dropbox.com/)

MEDIAFIRE

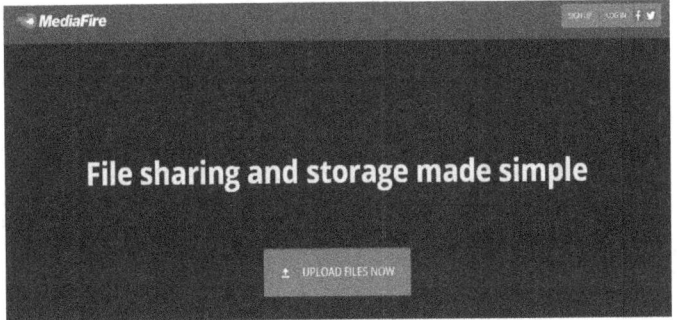

Know that with Mediafire sharing your files is the last thing you should worry about. Mediafire offers 10GB storage space and a 4GB file upload limit to all free users. Simply signup, upload your files, and send the links to who and where you want to send the files to. Mediafire also provides both android and iOS mobile apps for users to access their files anywhere and anytime.

(https://www.mediafire.com/)

ZIPPYSHARE

It is an act of omission if we fail to mention Zippyshare. This is a free file-sharing site with no upload and downloads limits, but you can only upload files not up to 500MB at once, and it will be removed after 30 days. You don't need to have an account with Zippyshare to use it. The only setback about this site is that it has no appealing interface.

(https://www.zippyshare.com/)

Chapter 10

AUTOMATION & INTEGRATION

Are you thinking of ways to automate your recurring tasks that take most of your valuable time during your marketing processes? There are some tools that will help you integrate apps and tools to work together, even if they are not supposed to do it. The best when it comes to automation and integration of your tasks are all tools mentioned below, but to enjoy it to the fullest, you have to go for the paid version. However, listed below are Zapier and some alternative tools to Zapier and are free to use.

ZAPIER

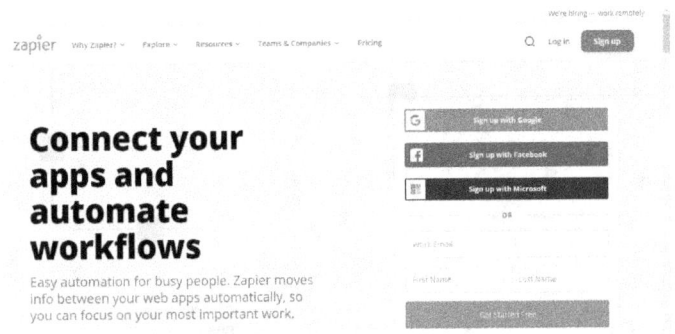

Zapier is the most trusted of all the online automation tools that help connect preferred apps that include MailChimp, Gmail, Slack, and more. It has become the best virtual assistant to all business owners that want to integrate apps and automate recurring tasks that will normally take time without any technical know-how. Zapier allows you to perform tasks by integrating apps to work together for a common goal. It comes in free and paid plans.

(https://zapier.com/)

INTEGROMAT

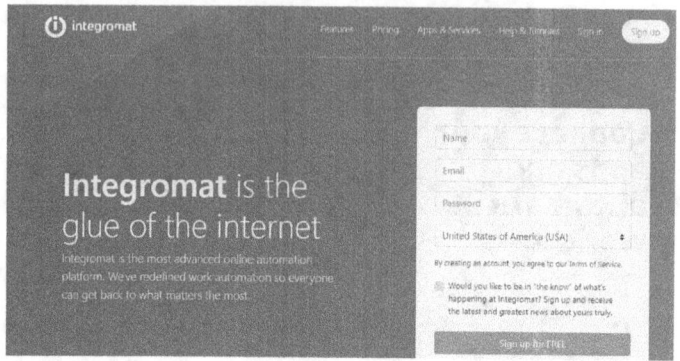

Integromat is one of the advanced online automation tools that helps more than 49000 companies integrate their services, apps, and systems. Its editor allows its user to create workflow without knowledge of coding. Integromat comes with hundreds of templates that will aid your setting up of workflow. It comes with free and paid plans. With the free plan, you have access to 1000 operations, 100 MB data transfer, and many more.

(https://www.integromat.com/en/)

AUTOMATE

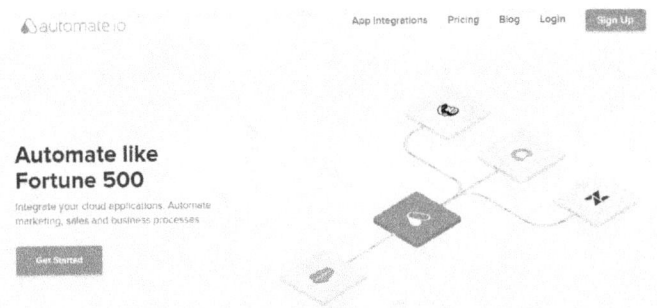

Automate is an excellent solution that helps business owners in integrating their cloud-based apps. With the Automate, you will create complex workflow (Bots) and automate your marketing sales, business strategies, and eCommerce. It is very easy to set Automate up as it has a user-friendly interface (drag and drop). The Automate allows you to create one-on-one integrations workflow within minutes, streamline sales strategies, automate your email, set up a functional internal workflow, social campaigns, and more. Automate comes in free and paid plans.

(https://automate.io/)

MICROSOFT FLOW

Take care of what's important.
Automate the rest.

Streamline repetitive tasks and paperless processes with Microsoft Power Automate—so you can focus your attention where it's needed most.

Microsoft Flow is an excellent and underrated automation tool and is known to always outshine Zapier. With this tool, you will be able to use different templates to create automated workflows between your apps and services, and many more. It comes with thousands of templates that will aid your creation of automation. These templates are organized in categories for easy identification; marketing, sales, teaching, HR, email, and more. Microsoft Flow comes from a free package to paid plans.

(https://flow.microsoft.com/en-us/)

Chapter 11

ANALYTICS & MARKET RESEARCH

There is no doubt that what differentiates a good business from a great one is the proper analysis and market research before embarking on projects. This is a fundamental and essential element to improve, evolve, and craft products and services that the market needs and wants. Selling is not about what you think people want to buy, but about what they need and want. Not only will the tools for Analytics and Market Research tell you what is selling, but they will also provide you details insights into your competitors, economic shifts, consumer buying patterns, demographics, and more.

The following tools will help you streamlining market research and provide valuable reports that will make you ride over your competitors.

BUZZSUMO

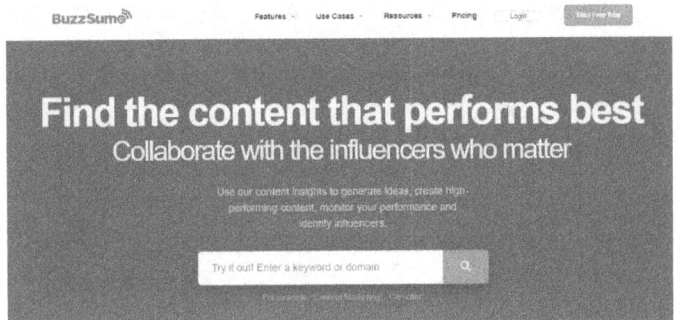

Buzzsumo is a tool that affords you to see engaging pieces of content and find new potential opportunities. With Buzzsumo, you will discover contents that are most liked, shared, and comments on. It will reveal your competitor's content performance for you to decipher. With the Buzzsumo analysis option, you will be able to see high-performing influencers in your niche, be able to monitor mentioning of your niche or brand, backlinks, and many more. All these features and others will help you and your team develop the best content, products, and services. It comes with a 30-day free trial and paid plans.

(https://buzzsumo.com/)

MOZ

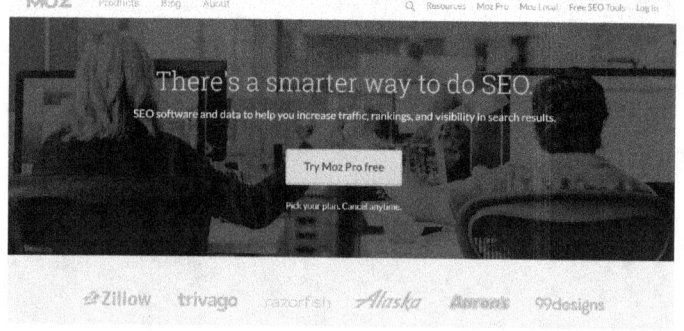

Moz, which is also SEO, is a powerful digital marketing tool that you can use to gain valuable traffic and convert into conversions. With Moz, you will be able to know about on-site and off-site optimization of any website. It will give you the data needed to increase your services or products' ranking results. Moz comes with 30 days of free trial that you can cancel anytime and paid plans.

(https://moz.com/)

GOOGLE ANALYTICS

Analytics

Welcome to Google Analytics

Google Analytics gives you the free tools you need to analyze data for your business in one place, so you can make smarter decisions.

Set up for free

Complete information

Understand your site and app users to better check the performance of your marketing, content, products, and more.

Get insights only Google can give

Access Google's unique insights and machine learning capabilities to make the most of your data.

Google Analytics is one of the most popular digital analytics platforms on the web. It is a Google-free web analytics tool that affords you the opportunity to analyze the in-depth details about people that visit your website. This Google free service will let you know who visit, the details of who visit, how long they stay on the site, and which of your website pages they stay longer. The insights it provides will make you shape the success plan of your brand. Presently the Google Analytics 360 costs $150,000 per year. Still, Google makes the free version to provide more than enough reports for small and medium-sized entrepreneurs to be able to successfully guide their brands.

(https://analytics.google.com/analytics/web/provision/#/provision)

GOOGLE TRENDS

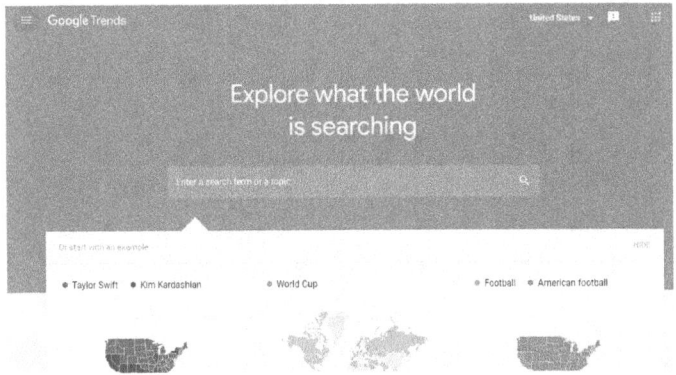

Google Trends is a search trend tool from Google that helps o display how frequent a particular search term is inputted into Google search engine relative to the site's total search volume over a specific period. The term to be searched can be in topics, phrases, and keywords. The results will help the content creators to know what people are searching for, and they will use the information to create content around the results gotten. Google Trends, like Google Analytics, is free to all users.

(https://trends.google.com/trends/?geo=US)

TYPEFORM

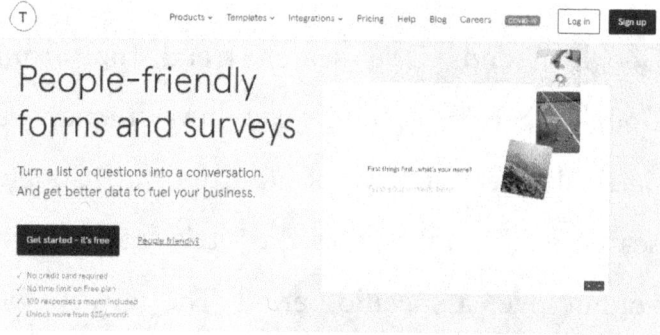

Typeform is a web platform to get real answers from followers, customers, or people from forms, quizzes, and surveys. The answers gotten will afford you the golden chance to improve your market research results and be able to create an excellent content strategy. Typeform comes in free and paid plans.

(https://www.typeform.com/)

Chapter 12

WEBINAR

The rapid development in technology has made it easy to establish communication with remote team members and customers. This development leads to organizing web conferences, which has gained popularity among entrepreneurs. With webinars, you promote your products, offer online training, business meetings, and more. It has become an essential ingredient in online marketing strategy.

ZOOM

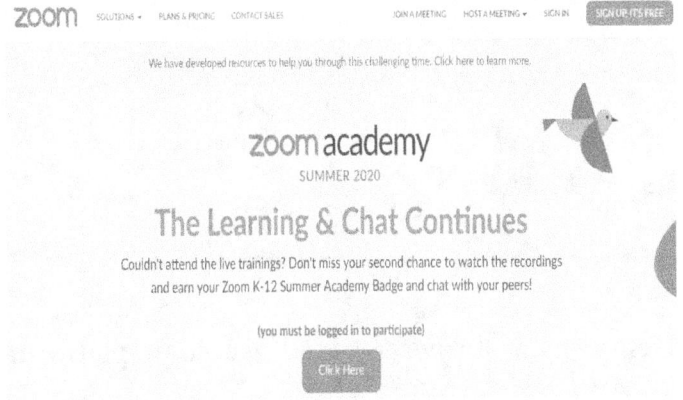

Zoom is presently the most popular of all the webinars. It comes with basic options for free for 40 minutes, and not more than 100 participants. With Zoom, you will have excellent video conferencing that includes screen sharing, annotations on the screen, group, and private chats. Zoom works on all devices and platforms.

(https://zoom.us/)

DEMIO

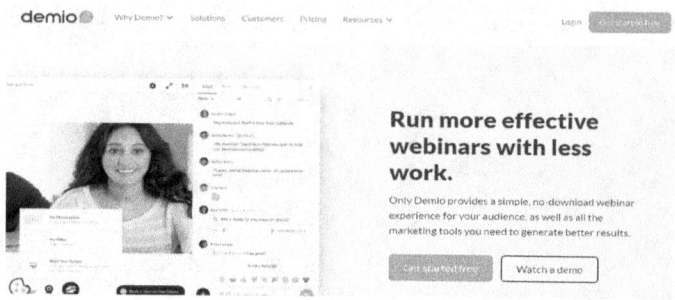

Demio is a browser-based webinar platform designed for business owners on a low budget, and it is to help make the engagements of the customers more powerful. It is designed with tracking and analytics options that will help you make the webinars, demonstrate products, and online training great. Demio will aid the automation of segmentation and let CTAs comes live to your audience. It comes with free and paid plans. However, the free comes with a 14-day free trial.

(https://demio.com/)

GOOGLE+ HANGOUTS

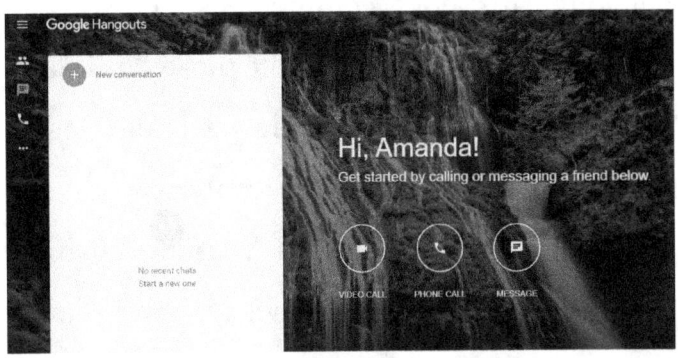

This is a video calling platform from Google, and it has been integrated with other Google tools such as Gmail, GChat, and Google calendar. Simply signup to a free Google account, and you are good to go. Though Google hangout is not regarded as a webinar, it is designed with some tools and options to accommodate collaborative meetings, workshops, and presentations. The only thing that makes it not a webinar is that Google has not incorporated into it the option to charge participants to hang out or sell while in the hangout. This tool accommodates ten people in a single audio/video call, while those on G-Suite can accommodate 25 people per call. Google hangout will allow you to connect your live stream to your website or Youtube channel, share your screen, be able to send emoji, chatting during the hangout, and it works on all platforms and devices.

(https://hangouts.google.com/)

WBINARJAM

Webinarjam is a cloud-based tool designed to help entrepreneurs and business owners create and conduct webinar sessions, such as live streaming on Youtube, Facebook, or via webinar rooms. It can be incorporated with other tools to create an automated follow-up strategy with the webinar, such as SMS, follow-up email, and many more. Webinarjam comes with a 30-day risk-free money-back guarantee.

(https://home.webinarjam.com/index?r_done=1)

SKYPE

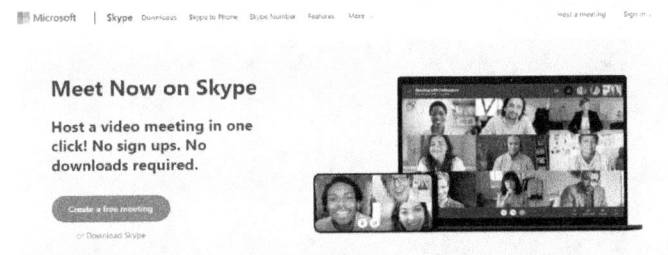

Discover more features

There is no doubt that Skype is one of the most popular video calling apps in the world. However, Skype is not a webinar due to its limitations. But if you are on a low budget and are a small business owner, you can use it to create and conduct some crucial business meetings with your customers. Skype allows group calls where 25 people can be in the group. It allows easy sharing of files and sharing of the screen.

(https://www.skype.com/en/)

Chapter 13

CALENDAR MANAGEMENT & APPOINTMENT SCHEDULING

Tasks like writing emails and coordination are some of the things that take up the most time of small business owners. However, tools that arrange appointments, scheduling, and booking will help them automate the processes with their existing and potential customers. These tools will speed up your sales process by allowing your prospects to book meetings and give you more time to running other areas of your business. Most of the tools discussed sync with the calendar and will send out the meeting reminders automatically.

CALENDLY

The Calendly comes in free and paid plans, but you can try all this tool features in 14 days. However, the free plan affords you the opportunity to book unlimited meetings, the ability to create a custom Calendly link, the ability to connect your calendar, and sending out the notifications and reminders to the participants. The disadvantage of the free plan is that you are limited to 1 type of meeting.

(https://calendly.com/)

DOODLE

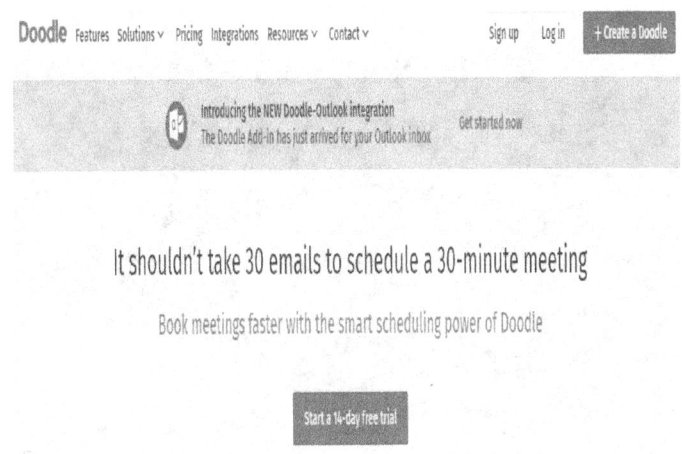

Once you sign up for Doodle's free plan, you will be able to create meeting polls to send to customers. As it is in the paid plan, the meeting will suggest meeting date and time, and the invitees will vote on the date and times to pick for the actual meeting.

(https://doodle.com/en/)

APPOINTLET

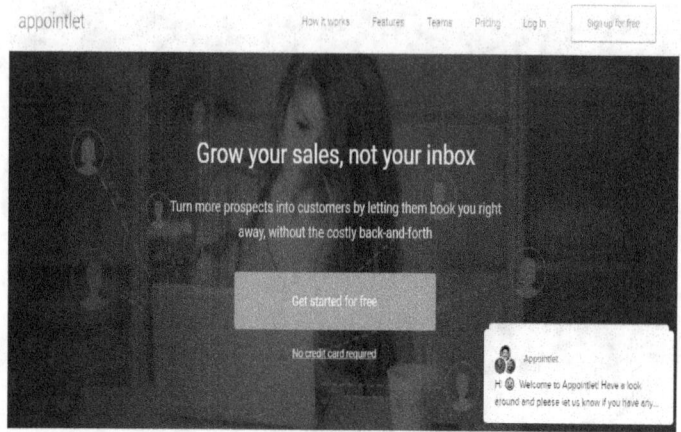

With this free booking appointment software, you will be able to customize your availability, create booking pages, and be able to send the booking pages to your customers and prospects. You can use the booking page to integrate into your website, emails, and landing pages.

Though it comes with free and paid plans but its free plan, do not expire.

(https://www.appointlet.com/)

SETMORE

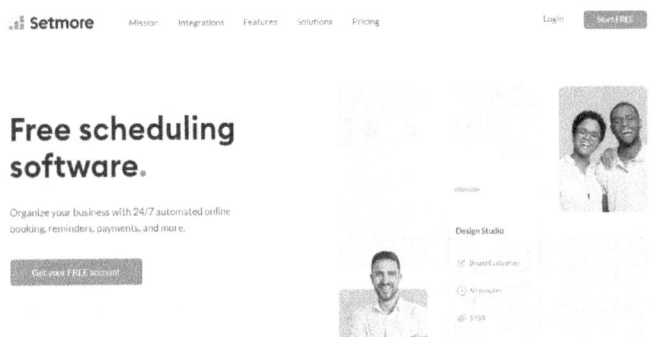

Setmore came in the free plan and paid plans that allow the business owners to create booking pages. The free plan allows you to add up to 4 staff calendars so that the team can start booking meetings. With this tool, you will send appointment notifications automatically to prospects who have booking times with you.

(https://www.setmore.com/)

Chapter 14

ECOMMERCE

Electronic Commerce, also known as eCommerce, is the buying and selling of goods, services, and digital products over the internet. Ecommerce has been known to be the goldmine of the internet. The services provided through eCommerce include money transactions, funds transactions, data transactions, and many more. Goods selling on eCommerce include mobile devices, health and fitness products, electronics, clothes, crafts, and many more. The following tools are in two categories- the first two are the best premium eCommerce platforms, and the last two are freemium with open-source platforms.

WIX

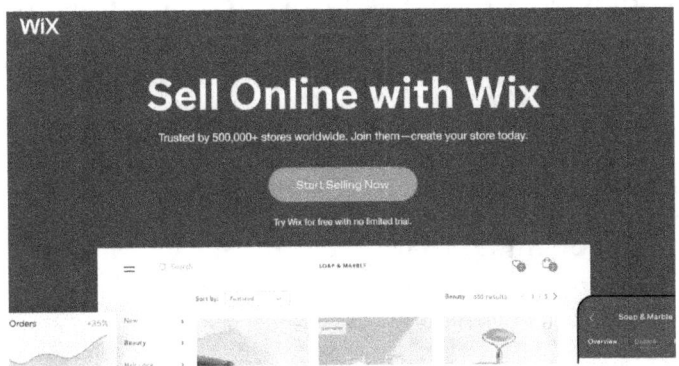

Wix is ranked to be the best eCommerce platform on the internet. Its primary task is to allow the customers to build a simple and straightforward website or an online store. We discovered that Wix had powered over 500,000 businesses all over the world. It has a hosting plan for the online store that people on a low budget can tap into. The hosting starts from $23 per month with an annual sub.

Wix comes with over 500 free mobile eCommerce themes and over 90 languages to build your online store. With this hosting plan, you can add an unlimited number of physical products to your store. You may try Wix for free with no limited trial.

(https://www.wix.com/mystunningwebsites/store -en?)

SHOPIFY

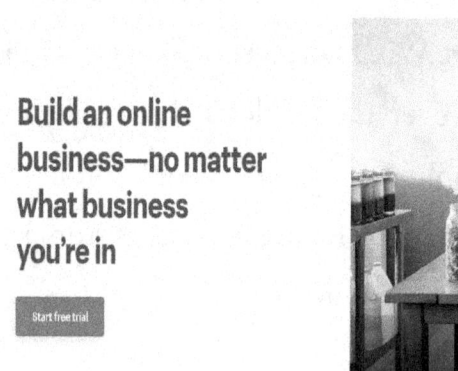

Shopify, no doubt, is the most popular eCommerce platform. It has over 1 million online stores, 2.1 million active users, and billions of dollars' worth of goods sold. There is a chance to start 14 days of a free trial, but their plan begins from $29 per month. Shopify has an in-house payment processor and great substantial discounts on its shipping rates. It comes with over 73 mobile-optimized themes that are stunningly beautiful. Out of these numbers, 64 are paid, and nine are free. There is no limit to the number of products you can display on your Shopify App Store.

(https://www.shopify.com/)

WOOCOMMERCE

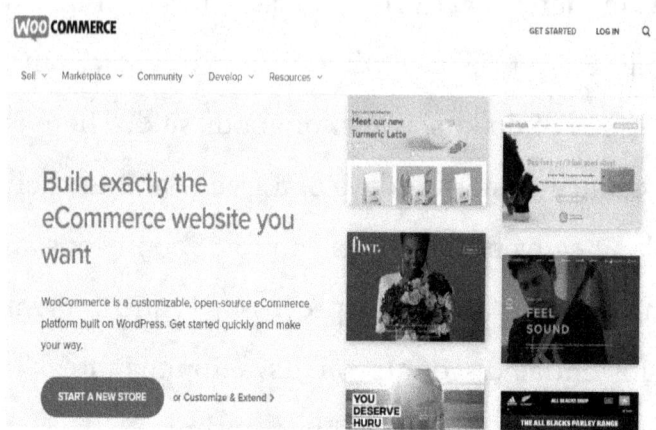

WooCommerce is one of the best free eCommerce platforms, but you will have to have gotten your web hosting and a domain name previously to make it free. You can now set up WooCommerce through your hosting web panel with the simple installation with these on hand.

WooCommerce is a free plugin from WordPress and is entirely free when you want to get started. However, there are paid extensions, themes, and integrations that you can add to your store to enhance its beauty and simplicity. It comes with many free themes that can be used to build an online store or buy some premium themes to make your store unique.

(https://woocommerce.com/)

OPENCART

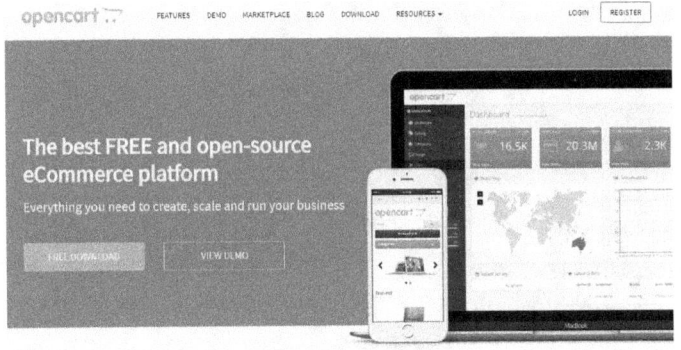

OpenCart is an open-source eCommerce platform that can only be fulfilled once you have gotten your hosting and a domain name.

It presently supports almost 400,000 eCommerce stores. OpenCart is designed with in-built options and a library of free extensions. It has a user-friendly mobile interface that comes with free and paid themes. OpenCart allows you to add unlimited products with both subscription and one-time selling plans on your online store.

(https://www.opencart.com/)

Chapter 15

PAYMENT PROCESSING

If you are services or goods provider, you will need a reputable payment processor that is acceptable and easy to use. You must have the one that is best for your business and has great customer care services. There are numerous of them on the web, but here are some of the best you can choose from, and are:

PAYPAL

There is no doubt that PayPal has proven to be one of the solid payment processors since its inception in 1989. Apart from having budget-friendly prices, PayPal is now being used in over 200 countries. It allows its user in adding PayPal checkout on their websites.

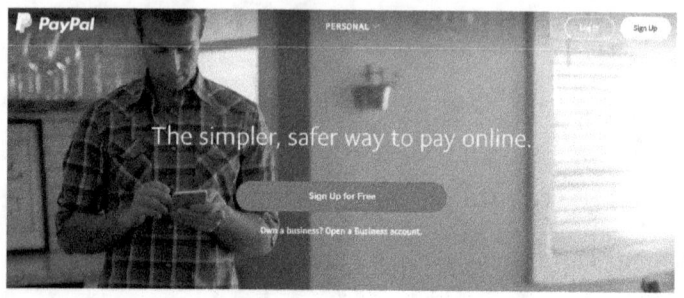

PayPal is for everyone who pays online.

(https://www.paypal.com/)

STRIPE

Stripe is another great payment processor for online retailers and developers who can use the Stripe APIs to create a product that will cater to their needs. It also allows you to accept bitcoin, debit, and credit payment on your website from over 130 currencies. Stripe billing is 2.9% + 30¢ for any successful card charge.

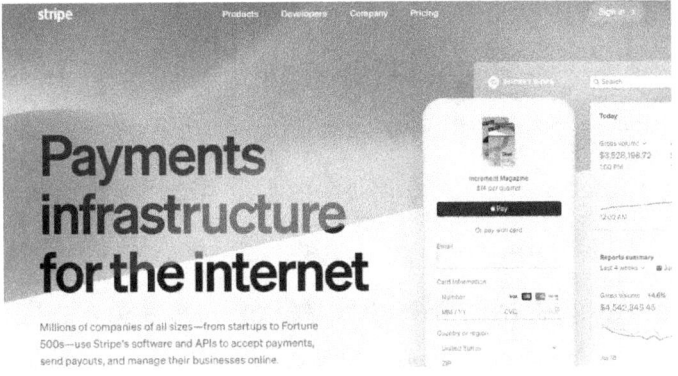

(https://stripe.com/)

BITPAY

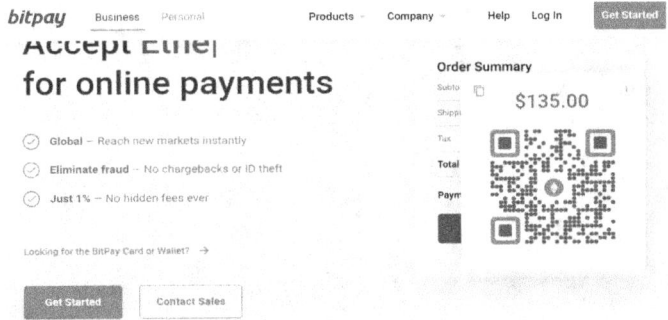

BitPay is the largest bitcoin payment processor and was founded in 2011. There is a claimed web that BitPay is responsible for more than $1 million in bitcoin transactions every day. With BitPay, you will convert bitcoin payment into your chosen currency from the nine currencies available on their 38 countries site. BitPay has partnered with Merchant Acquirers and PayPal to easy the form of payment.

(https://bitpay.com/)

GOCARDLESS

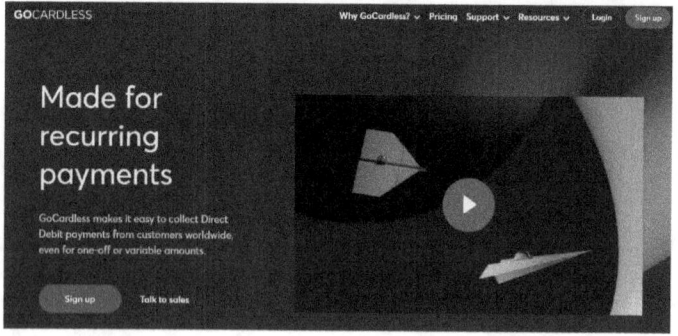

With this provider, you don't need any card to make your payment. GoCardless is a reputable online direct debit provider, their payments are easy to set up, and you can make payments automatic, track it, and integrate their services on your site. Billing on this platform is 1% in the United Kingdom and Europe, while it is 2% international.

(https://gocardless.com/)

Chapter 16

INSTANT MESSAGING

If you are an entrepreneur and probably using instant messengers on your devices for social or personal things only, you are missing. Instant messaging is one of the beauties of communication in this era. Instant messaging will stand in the gap when you have not gained all the necessary experience to write convertible emails as support to your customers. Instant messaging offers you the ability to communicate with your clients anytime without losing context. It affords you the opportunity of getting to know them more.

Also, some other instant messengers are not for customers, but the teams are internal instant messengers. Below are some for the external (customers) use and internal (team) use.

WHATSAPP BUSINESS

Whatsapp is a newcomer to instant messaging for business, but it comes with lots of potentials that will make marketing and customer support awesome. Whatsapp offers two types of IM app for business; Business App for small business and Business API for enterprise IM. Presently, Whatsapp has dominated consumer markets in Europe and Latin America. So it is recommended as it has over 1.3 billion users. This IM is for external use.

TELEGRAM

Don't lose the chance of connecting with some chunk of over 200 million active users on telegram. If you are in a country where messaging tools are tightly enforced, we will advise you to choose telegram. Another benefit of telegram over Whatsapp is that telegram allows over 100,000 people in a group. This is also an external IM.

SLACK

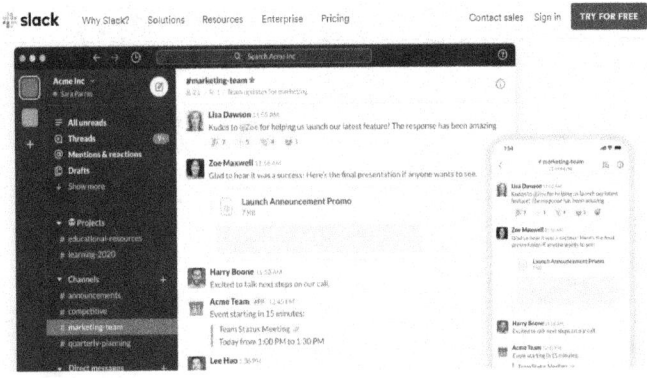

When it comes to the champion of IM for business, Slack is the one. Slack provides 1-on-1 and group chat functions for your business if you are an SME. With Slack, you will be able to archive 10,000 messages. Your files are searchable, and chats are synced on Slack as you don't have to worry your team members every time for files and chats. This tool is for the internal IM.

(https://slack.com/intl/en-ng/features)

Chapter 17

ENTREPRENEUR PODCASTS

With several resources in the form of podcasts available on the internet to the entrepreneurs on how to be successful, business owners have made starting up not a blind game again. Though there are many ways to learn from successful founders of businesses, we have seen that one of the best ways to learn is by listening to these founders and online creators' podcasts.

Below is a list of the great podcast for entrepreneurs. All the podcasts below are free.

TIM FERRISS SHOW

Tim Ferriss is the bestselling author of the 4-Hour Workweek, a book that has been translated to over 40 languages. His show, named The Tim Ferriss Show, has gone above 200 million downloads. He specializes in digging deep into knowing the tools, strategy, and tricks for his listeners to discern their success tips.

(https://tim.blog/podcast/)

GARYVEE AUDIO EXPERIENCE

WELCOME TO THE GARYVEE AUDIO EXPERIENCE

SUBSCRIBE HERE:

This is a show hosted and organized by entrepreneur, CEO, Vlogger, investor, and speaker Gary Vaynerchuk. His podcasts specialize in marketing, business, interviews, and fresh ideas on how to.

(https://www.garyvaynerchuk.com/podcast/)

ENTREPRENEURS ON FIRE

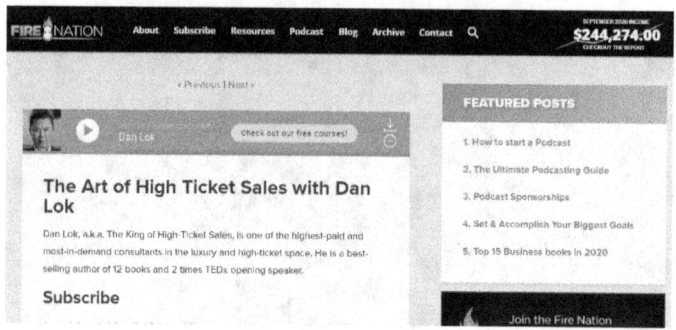

This is a daily interview podcast that focuses on entrepreneurs and business owners' journey from their entrepreneurial experience to their Eureka moments. The founder of Entrepreneur on Fire, John Lee Dumas, stated that this platform is the best for you if you are tired of spending 90% of your day doing what you don't like doing. JLD, as he is fondly called, said his goal is to deliver the inspiration and strategies needed to fire up you into your entrepreneurial journey and be able to create the kind of life you want.

(https://www.eofire.com/podcast/danlok/)

SIDE HUSTLE SCHOOL

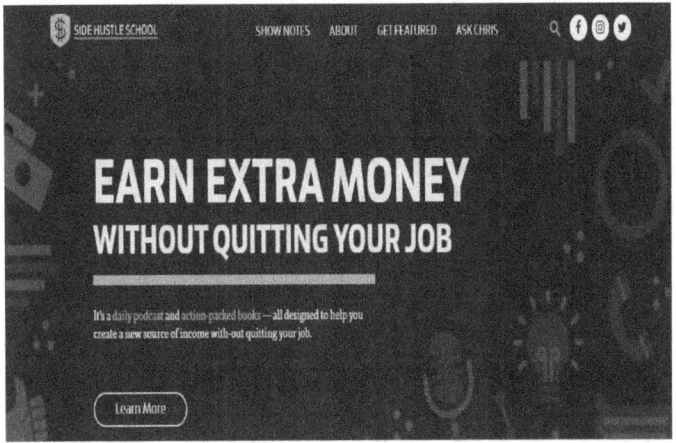

The Side Hustle School is designed for anyone who works a normal job and decides to start a side hustle. The school presents episodes where their listeners will hear the various story of people who have undergone what they just want to start-their challenges and how they overcame them. The show's anchor is Chris

Guillebeau, a bestselling author of The $100 StartUp and other books.

(https://sidehustleschool.com/)

MARKETING SCHOOL

In The Marketing School, Neil Patel and Eric Siu present daily well-researched marketing lessons they have acquired while growing up as entrepreneurs. This is a must school for those that want to learn how to bring their brands to the next level.

(http://mschool.growtheverywhere.libsynpro.com
/podcast)

YOUPRENEUR

Chris Ducker presents what it means to be a
personal brand entrepreneur in this 21st century
on this platform. Other lessons include how to
delegate, how to create and launch online

products and services, how to market yourself in your chosen industry.

(https://www.chrisducker.com/)

CONCLUSION

Thank you for buying this book!

I'm happy that you have made it to the end of this handbook.

There is no denying the fact that remote work has come to stay while its growth is being recorded every day. With the growth in the number of remote work, it has become very easy to own and operate an online business.

We have covered some groundbreaking chapters that have to do with free tools every entrepreneur should have. The information dished out was created to teach you how to use the tools and expose you to tools that will make you excel in your day to day activities

These tools will help you save time, energy, and money on recurring tasks that engage and exhaust you daily.

Look no further and start using this book to Build Trust, Communication, Projects, Business Growth, and Inspiration to Leap forward.

Congratulations! As you make good use of this book.

Thanks.

References

https://www.wordstream.com/blog/ws/2018/01/17/best-free-social-media-management-tools

https://crm.org/crmland/free-crm

https://www.timedoctor.com/blog/outsourcing-websites/

https://solutionsreview.com/marketing-automation/

https://themeisle.com/blog/free-zapier-alternatives/